Cryptocurrency:
How to Make Money from it?

10 True and Tried Ways

Your Free Gift

Best Crypto Resources inside

Online Courses

High Quality Blogs

Markets

Hardware wallet (best security)

My wallet recommendations

List of all cryptocurrencies

Charts

Calendars ICO

Top twitter accounts of the crypto industry

Email newsletter

Podcasts

Best Global Forum

Statistics on ICO

Table of Contents

Introduction 5

Chapter 1 - What Are Cryptocurrencies? 7

Chapter 2 - Mining 9

    How does mining work? 9

Chapter 3 - Cloud Mining 13

Chapter 4 - Trading 14

Chapter 5 - Buy and Hold 16

Chapter 6 - Coinflash 17

Chapter 7 - Selling goods for Cryptocurrency 18

Chapter 8 - Cryptocurrency Faucets 20

Chapter 9 - Working online for Cryptocurrency Payments 22

Chapter 10 - Gambling 23

Chapter 11 - Become a lender 24

Conclusion 26

Great Bonus – Crypto Resources 28

    Markets: 28

    Hardware Wallet (Best Security): 28

    My Wallet Recommendations: 28

    List of All Cryptocurrencies: 29

    Chart 29

    Calendars ICO: 29

    Twitter: 29

    Bots: 31

    Email-lists: 32

    Podcasts 32

Best Global Forum 32
Statistics on ICO 32
Online Courses: 33
High Quality Blogs: 33

Introduction

When anyone of has some money lying around unused for long they either decide to put it in a bank account in order to receive interest on it or else they start to list the opportunities they can exploit using that money. Traditionally, people go for stock options, Forex, or maybe real estate when the amount is big enough. In late years, though, one investment option has been beating at every aspect any other scenario someone with liquidity can invest their money in. This investment option is what came to be known as a cryptocurrency. With very low initial investments, people have been able to generate massive amounts of money trading cryptocurrency over the past few years.

There are many misconceptions around cryptocurrency trading that, although having emerged at times when the business was still in its initial phases, still persist despite its exponential growth in recent years. One above all is the idea that cryptocurrency is this shady, fraudulent industry rather than an official and prosperous business that has become a central (and the most growing) part of the financial industry worldwide as of late. This book aims to challenge such misconceptions, introduce you to the endless possibilities of cryptocurrency trading, and get you familiar with the ten most reliable ways to flourish in that business even if you are still starting up.

Chapter 1 - What Are Cryptocurrencies?

The name Bitcoin and the term cryptocurrency have both been used interchangeably and constantly mistaken for one another for many years. Because of its popularity, as well as the fact that it was the first and that it was for years the sole big player in the cryptocurrency arena, Bitcoin became synonymous with cryptocurrency. The truth is, Bitcoin is but one currency among a plethora of digital and cryptocurrencies that exist today. So, what exactly are cryptocurrencies?

These are digital currencies that do not fall under the umbrella of conventional fiat currencies. They are decentralized mediums of exchange that are initialized by private companies, managed through public ledgers (Ex: blockchain in the case of Bitcoin) that are run and verified by random users who volunteer to undertake this role. Cryptocurrencies are money units that are represented by digital entries into that network or public ledger. For the sake of privacy, but at the same time to enable the verification of transactions, cryptocurrencies are issued under pseudonyms that cover up the identities of both parties to a transaction. Bitcoin, which is considered the first actual decentralized digital currency, was issued in 2009 by a person with the pseudonym Satoshi Nakamoto who remains unknown to this day. Since then, dozens of other cryptocurrencies have been set up and launched into the digital space. Some of the most well-known among them at the moment are Ethereum (second strongest cryptocurrency after Bitcoin), MadeSafeCoin, NEM, Dash, and Ripple.

If you are just starting to get a grasp on how real and enormous the cryptocurrency industry is, then you probably are not yet aware of a number of experts specialized today in studying just that industry. I am not talking low-key figures with little credibility, but rather real financial and economic experts working for large capital firms and organizations. That is only proportional to the massive value cryptocurrencies have come to represent. When Bitcoin started back in 2009, the Bitcoin currency held little to no value. Tens of bitcoins held virtually the same worth as some pennies. As of September 2017, however, one Bitcoin is worth around $4,000, and the overall market cap of Bitcoin is almost $70 billion. That is only one of the currencies.

The purpose of this book will be to take you through ten of the most prominent methods to enter into the cryptocurrency arena and be able to generate income. The available methods are actually countless, but these are arguably the most guaranteed and reliable of them all. Let us start. ☐

Chapter 2 - Mining

You can basically think of mining as the crypto equivalent to money-printing. With traditional currencies, central banks decide when to print cash and when to hold back. With cryptocurrencies, this process too is decentralized, and therefore anyone can become a Bitcoin miner using the necessary equipment.

How does mining work?

Although most people when discussing cryptocurrency mining tend to refer to Bitcoin, they do not necessarily mean Bitcoin. As confusing as that is, Bitcoin is still used as a catchall name for pretty much all of the cryptocurrencies out there. Only lately has the term "altcoin" emerged to refer to alternatives to Bitcoin (most popular among them is Ethereum.) First off, you need to know that as a cryptocurrency miner, your job is not merely to issue new currency, but even more importantly, you serve to verify transactions made by other people on the blockchain.

What a miner needs to kick start their "mining station" as we might call it, is a powerful computer (a mining rig) with high processing power and an advanced graphics card. This high-end equipment is necessary because it will be needed to solve complex algorithms. This is the cornerstone of cryptocurrency mining. Take Bitcoin as an example. New Bitcoins are issued when your computer (as a miner,) through solving these algorithms, is able to come up with a new hash. It is compared to pre-existing hashes (which represent the Bitcoins,) and if no similar hash already exists, then you would have practically "mined" a new coin. That means that you added a new Bitcoin to the global Bitcoin network.

After having issued that coin, you get to keep it. What you then do is add it to your cryptocurrency wallet, and from that point on, it is all yours. You can use it to make purchases online from channels that accept cryptocurrency, or as most miners tend to do, you can trade it for a conventional currency like USD or GBP.

You do not necessarily have to dedicate all of your resources to mining a single cryptocurrency. While some choose to do so, it is not exactly the most efficient way to go about your mining business. That is because cryptocurrency is a super volatile arena, meaning that the opportunity cost of mining one currency over another could change by the day with the fluctuation occurring in each respective currency. It might be more profitable for you to mine Bitcoins today considering the mining costs against the potential return, but your best bet tomorrow might rather be on Ethereum. Because it is definitely no simple job (especially as an individual miner) to be constantly monitoring and studying your investment options, there is software like NiceHash Miner whose main function is to allocate your processing power to the algorithms that are most profitable at the moment. Such software substantially increases your mining efficiency, and so it is always a smart decision to invest some money in buying it. You need to be aware, though, that such software usually pays you in a particular cryptocurrency. For example, NiceHash Miner pays you only in Bitcoin.

The main risk in mining is that of saturation. Cryptocurrencies tend to have a ceiling on a number of coins that are to enter its global network. For example, Bitcoins are set to stop being produced when 21 million Bitcoins are already in circulation. After that, no one will be able to mine anymore Bitcoins. This means that, as more people get in on the mining activity for a particular cryptocurrency, the new hashes or blocks waiting to be mined will decrease. That means that your opportunity to be the one who mines them will in turn decrease, thus giving you a lower "hash rate."

Mining pays off quite well for those who live in countries where electricity is cheap, which is mostly in developing countries. That is because the mining process, with all the computing activity it requires 24/7, ends up consuming massive amounts of electric power. If you live in a country where utilities come at a steep price, then this might not be your best option for making money off cryptocurrency. Sometimes people who live in developed countries decide to get into the mining business, and so they head to some developing country (some of the most common destinations are in East Asia) to set up a mining station there in order to benefit from the low utility costs. Of course, despite the low operation costs, the initial investment tends to be quite high. You probably would not cross oceans and borders to another country to set up a mining station running a single computer. It has to be worth the hectic logistics. □

Chapter 3 - Cloud Mining

Cloud mining is a less hectic alternative to owning a mining rig. You get to invest some of your money into a shared mining station. A service provider sets up a mining center, manages the equipment and the utilities that go into the mining process, and all you are required to do is pay them a fee for your share in the mining equipment. Then you get to profit from the outcome of the mining based on your share. The main advantage of cloud mining is that you do not need to endure the whole hassle of buying the hardware, running the equipment with all the electricity that the process consumes, and having to suffer from the heat generated from the computers due to the excessive processing power that goes into mining. Somebody else handles all of this for you and all you do is you invest your money from afar. The downside of this is that the cost is higher than if you set up your very own mining center. That is because you are paying management costs to whoever is providing the service. You also have less control over the mining process. However, if you place more value on comfort and do not mind your profit margin being diminished by the management costs, then this is a somewhat safe and easy way to go.☐

Chapter 4 - Trading

This is considered the gist of the matter when it comes to cryptocurrency. You can make money from many sources, but the big bucks in fairly short periods are made in the trading venue. Speculation on digital currency has earned people millions. However, although it carries the greatest potential between the other methods, it also carries with it the highest risk and demands more effort than anything else. Just like Forex or stock trading, cryptocurrency involves a good amount of research. First, you need to know which currencies are hot on the market right now. That entails you going on cryptocurrency-related forums and groups to get a feel of the market's pulse. You need to know what is on the rise, why it is on the rise, whether that rise is expected to persist for a while or if it is just a bubble that is soon to burst up like many fear with Bitcoin at the moment, and which of the underdog currencies is expected to make it to the cryptocurrency stratosphere in the near future so you can get in early on and benefit from the boom. All this information will require a fair amount of reading and monitoring on a daily basis.

When getting into cryptocurrency trading, you also want to educate yourself about the laws in your country or a particular city. The regulations concerning cryptocurrencies are still not mature enough because the industry is yet in its infancy phase, and so they are prone to change, both in favor or against, your trading business at any time. In both cases, you need to be well-prepared and equipped with enough knowledge to know just when to go in and when to pull out. Although it might involve more effort than most cryptocurrency money-making methods, trading definitely pays off in the end if you approach it professionally like a big investor would deal with their stock portfolio. Every piece of news is relevant, every change in the system deserves scrutiny, and trends need to be detected and acted upon in their very first stages or even before they actually go into action.

You cannot expect to get the hang of this whole business when you are only starting out. There will always be more to learn, but just like with anything else, you will only learn if you throw yourself out there and get into the action. However, you want to go about this the smart way, so you do not want to learn with all your money. That is why you should start small, get to learn with the bits you invest in the beginning, and as you acquire more knowledge and trading savvy, you can start putting in more money and thus get a higher return on investment. The best way to go about this is to have everything planned at the outset, and only alter your plan when something new emerges. ☐

Chapter 5 - Buy and Hold

Besides short-term cryptocurrency trading, there are entrepreneurs who stay on the lookout for new digital currencies that are just starting up. Cryptocurrencies are initiated in what is called an ICO or an initial coin offering. Most cryptocurrencies start off with minimal prices per coin, but those that rise can get to astronomical prices in a brief period of time. You can ask people who acquired Bitcoins when they were selling for just a few dollars and are now millionaires after just a few years with every Bitcoin they own being worth north of $4,000 as I write these words. There are other currencies that were launched in very recent years and are now trading at very decent prices (Ex: Ethereum - $290, Dash - $300+, Monero - $90+) and have made fortunes for those who acquired them in their early days. There are now currencies like Ripple and NEM that are trading at lower than $0.5 per coin. With the right research and a good eye for opportunities, you can very well be investing in a currency with a future market cap of more than $1 billion. It takes you time to harvest the gains from such a strategy, but if you approach it the right way, your small investment could be turned into a pretty massive wealth within a few years. □

Chapter 6 - Coinflash

Coinflash is a smartphone app that just recently launched. This app is a good tool to use in order to profit from cryptocurrency without worrying much about the whole process. What you basically do with this app is link it to your credit or debit card, and with every purchase, the app rounds the value you pay to the nearest dollar and automatically invests the change into a cryptocurrency of your choice. That way, without you giving it much thought, you are investing little bits of your money into cryptocurrency that will eventually build up into a decent wallet. Do not underestimate what that change can get you because many of the currencies that are still in their initial phases cost less than a dollar per coin like we mentioned earlier. The wallet you build up can either be used for short-term trading when there is enough cryptocurrency in it to earn you a significant amount of profit or even better, you can allocate it to a buy and hold strategy and leave it to build up for long-term gain. ☐

Chapter 7 - Selling goods for Cryptocurrency

Like with any currency, you can acquire cryptocurrencies through providing goods or services.

Today you can become an exclusively cryptocurrency-paid online merchant. There is no limit to what is bought and sold for cryptocurrency right now. You can sell everything, from apparel to gadgets to even houses in exchange for Bitcoins or any other cryptocurrency. That could be done through your own platform, be it a website, a blog, or even a Facebook page where customers could pay you in cryptocurrency through any of the many platforms that facilitate this. You can also run your business through one of the online marketplaces that use cryptocurrency as the main medium of exchange. An example of such platforms is Bitify, which is now considered the Ebay for cryptocurrencies. You get to display your products on it, and an auction is run on them and the final price is paid in cryptocurrency. Many people who are unfamiliar with the world of cryptocurrency may think such platforms are not all that safe, but as a matter of fact, Bitify provides all forms of protection to its users, including escrow services to guarantee that customers receive their products before they release the payment. There are many other such platforms, so we can say with confidence that you have many marketplaces where you can offer your goods for cryptocurrency that you can add to your wallet either for saving or to trade when the time is right. □

Chapter 8 - Cryptocurrency Faucets

This might not be the most prominent or profitable way to make money with cryptocurrency, but it is a way to put your hands on a small amount without committing any resources. Basically, these faucets are websites for which you do simple services for a modest payout in Bitcoin or any other cryptocurrency. Most faucet websites are either concerned with raising their traffic in order to sell ad placements or promoting digital currency. In the case of the advertisement being the website's core revenue source, it would be willing to pay you a portion of that revenue in return for you viewing these ads and perhaps filling in some surveys afterward. Examples of such faucets are BestFaucet, TopFaucet, BTC Clicks and Bitcoin Aliens.

The other type of cryptocurrency faucets mainly concerned with promoting digital currencies would give you small fractions of a currency as a safe trial for you without you having to invest your money in it. These websites usually aim to get you in the cryptocurrency trading business and so they offer you these samples for you to use as a demo and get comfortable with the idea of using cryptocurrency. There are also other types of cryptocurrency faucets that offer lottery and betting services, and also a few where you can earn some coins from referring your friends to the website.

Faucets usually pay users in units called Satoshis. One Satoshi is a hundredth of a millionth of one Bitcoin. Pretty small, but they can add up to something worthwhile after you pile up a decent amount in your wallet depending on the rates at which the currency is selling. Of course, the return will never be anything close to that of trading or mining, but yet again, we are talking about a zero-capital activity, so you should not expect to hit the jackpot with it. It could be, however, your first step into the cryptocurrency venue.

While a safe bet would be to go on one or many of those faucet websites looking to earn a few Satoshis, you can also invest in building up your own cryptocurrency faucet website. By building a luring referral scheme and a well-to-do compensation plan for your users, you can enjoy an exponential growth in your website's traffic which you could then sell for ad revenues. □

Chapter 9 - Working online for Cryptocurrency Payments

There are websites and smartphone apps through which you can offer your services for a payment in Bitcoin or any other altcoin. These services include testing applications, watching videos, filling surveys, trying out online games, and many other possible micro-tasks. You can think of apps like Bituro, Coinbucks, and Bitcoin Rewards as the cryptocurrency counterparts of freelancing services platforms like Freelancer or Upwork.

There are other platforms that are even more like Freelancer and Upwork, meaning that you get to offer your services in many fields like web development, content writing, etc., through them in exchange for cryptocurrency payments. BitGigs and Coinality are examples of such sites. You go on them, you bid for projects that you think you can get done, and you get paid in Bitcoins or any altcoin.

Chapter 10 - Gambling

This chapter handles two of the more risky methods, but ones that have proven capable to generate sizable amounts of income.

If you are into any type of gambling, say poker, roulette, or blackjack, there are now platforms where you can get your gambling winnings in Bitcoin or other cryptocurrencies. You can go on online sites like Starcoin, Crypto Games, or vDice, set up an account and let the dice roll. This method definitely has the potential to add big sums of cryptocurrency to your wallet, but that, of course, requires some luck on your side, as well as some experience with gambling strategy. If you are confident with taking that risk and trust your savvy on a gambling table, you can end up with a fat cryptocurrency wallet in your possession. You can switch your games from the other online platforms to a cryptocurrency-paying alternative and test your luck. You will find cryptocurrency gambling platforms that are just as big as their fiat counterparts and can satisfy all your gambling urges.

Chapter 11 - Become a lender

Here is a solid example of where the decentralized nature of cryptocurrency comes into play. If you own a cryptocurrency wallet, trading is not your only way to use your coins. You can also become a lender. In the world of cryptocurrency, that does not require millions like it does with fiat currencies. Whatever your worth is, you can still become a lender for individuals or even SMEs trying to fund their business with cryptocurrency. There are even platforms like Bitbond that are specialized platforms in peer-to-peer cryptocurrency lending where you can meet potential clients searching for loans that you can provide for an interest.

The reason many startups and SMEs turn toward peer-to-peer loans is that it takes off their backs the burdens banks put on them with their endless obstacles. They are able to acquire a loan easier, and at the same time, you as a person with a decent cryptocurrency wallet can benefit from the interest you will impose on the loan. Such platforms simply made it easier for people to become both lenders and borrowers.

That simplicity, though, does not take off your back the responsibility of carefully considering your risks. If you turn towards peer-to-peer lending, you are probably not in possession of a huge amount of cryptocurrency. You need to fastidiously study your options and rationally decide who you are going to lend. Diversification is also a must. Many people fall into the mistake of investing their whole wallet's worth into one borrower and if that person or enterprise defaults on the loan, you are left with pretty much nothing. That is why it is always wise to lend several individuals or companies so that the risk of your overall investment is balanced.

☐

Conclusion

Hopefully, by now you have found one or methods which you are willing to invest yourself into in order to seize one of the many opportunities that cryptocurrency has to offer. Now is definitely the right time to enter this booming and prosperous industry as long as you have the resources to do so. Always keep in mind, though, that cryptocurrency is a legitimate business where you have to put in the work and research in order to harvest the great gains that you can make out of it. People who approach cryptocurrency with the professional mindset of an entrepreneur are the ones who get to walk away with large sums of money, whereas those who treat it too lightly and think of it as a get-rich-quick scheme do not go a long way and some even end up losing their investments. As I mentioned at the beginning of this book, this industry has its experts and requires proper financial knowledge, so a professional and scientific approach is essential to succeeding in it.

@ Copyright 2017 by Isaak Stark - All rights reserved.

All rights Reserved. No part of this publication or the information in it may be quoted from or reproduced in any form by means such as printing, scanning, photocopying or otherwise without prior written permission of the copyright holder.

Disclaimer and Terms of Use: Effort has been made to ensure that the information in this book is accurate and complete, however, the author and the publisher do not warrant the accuracy of the information, text and graphics contained within the book due to the rapidly changing nature of science, research, known and unknown facts and internet. The Author and the publisher do not hold any responsibility for errors, omissions or contrary interpretation of the subject matter herein. This book is presented solely for motivational and informational purposes only.

Great Bonus – Crypto Resources

Markets:

Poloniex

Bittrex

Kraken

Bitfinex

Hardware Wallet (Best Security):

Trezor

Keepkey

Ledger Nano S

My Wallet Recommendations:

Desktop wallet: Electrum

Android wallet: Samourai Wallet

iPhone wallet: breadwallet

Web wallet: BitGo

List of All Cryptocurrencies:

Coinmarketcap

https://www.cryptocompare.com/

Chart

http://tradingview.com/

Calendars ICO:

http://ico-list.com

https://tokenmarket.net/ico-calendar

Twitter:

https://twitter.com/aantonop

https://twitter.com/NickSzabo4

https://twitter.com/AlunaCrypto

https://twitter.com/satoshi_fund

https://twitter.com/CointraderGuy

https://twitter.com/whalecalls

https://twitter.com/alistairmilne

https://twitter.com/barrysilbert

https://twitter.com/ToneVays

https://twitter.com/cryptoSqueeze

https://twitter.com/jackfru1t

https://twitter.com/CollinCrypto

https://twitter.com/ThisIsNuse

https://twitter.com/petertoddbtc

https://twitter.com/anondran

https://twitter.com/bbands

https://twitter.com/a_l_e_c_o

https://twitter.com/maguraaa

https://twitter.com/CryptoSky

https://twitter.com/ActualAdviceBTC

https://twitter.com/SatoshiLite

https://twitter.com/WhalePanda

https://twitter.com/Excellion

https://twitter.com/21xhipster

https://twitter.com/IOHK_Charles

https://twitter.com/cypherdisco

https://twitter.com/jazzycrypt

https://twitter.com/CryptOrca

https://twitter.com/cnLedger

https://twitter.com/bobbyclee

https://twitter.com/gavofyork

https://twitter.com/onemanatatime

Bots:

https://twitter.com/AltcoinLiveBot

https://twitter.com/cryptocoinradar

https://twitter.com/AltcoinNotify

Email-lists:

https://CryptoCompare.com (sign up, they have good daily mailings)

Podcasts

Blockchain Dynamicsthe (best podcast about news crypto-markets, you can find it in any podcast player)

Unchained

Blockgeekslab

Best Global Forum

https://bitcointalk.org

Statistics on ICO

https://www.tokendata.io/

Online Courses:

In-depth Udemy Course (over 8 hours of video tutorials)

Coursera Cryptocurrency Course (61 videos in 11 sections)

Khan Academy Bitcoin Course (9 ~10 minute videos)

Bitcoin 101 Blackboard Series (7+ hours of tutorials)

Introduction to Bitcoin (create a free trial)

Introduction to Digital Currency - MOOC offered by

High Quality Blogs:

Bitcoin Tech Talk (Various)

Bitslog (Sergio Demian Lerner)

The Control (Nick Tomaino)

Eric Lombrozo

Financial Cryptography (Ian Grigg)

Fred Wilson

Freedom to Tinker

Gavin Andresen

Hacking, Distributed (Emin Gün Sirer)

Jimmy Song

JP Koning

Matt Corallo

The Memory Pool (Satoshi Nakamoto Institute)

Money and State (Erik Voorhees)

Nicolas Dorier

Oleg Andreev

Peter Todd

Richard Gendal Brown

Tim Swanson

Truthcoin (Paul Sztorc)

Tuur Demeester

Unenumerated (Nick Szabo)

Vinny Lingham

Willy Woo

Wladimir van der Laan

www.ingramcontent.com/pod-product-compliance
Lightning Source LLC
Chambersburg PA
CBHW050034230526
45470CB00003B/1270